A Baby Doesn't Make the Man:

Alternative Sources of Power
and
Manhood for Young Men

Teens may learn different ideas about masculinity by talking with their peers.

The Teen Pregnancy Prevention Library

A Baby Doesn't Make the Man:

Alternative Sources of Power and Manhood for Young Men

Raymond Jamiolkowski

THE ROSEN PUBLISHING GROUP, INC.
NEW YORK

Published in 1997 by The Rosen Publishing Group, Inc.
29 East 21st Street, New York, NY 10010

First Edition
Copyright © 1997 by The Rosen Publishing Group, Inc.

Manufactured in the United States of America.

Library of Congress Cataloging-in-Publication Data

Jamiolkowski, Raymond.
    A baby doesn't make the man: alternative sources of power and
manhood for young men / by Raymond Jamiolkowski.
        p.   cm. — (Teen pregnancy prevention library)
    Includes bibliographical references and index.
    Summary: Discusses reasons why teenage boys engage in sex, the
consequences of irresponsible sexual activity, and alternative ways for
young men to feel good about themselves.
    ISBN 0-8239-2251-0
    1. Sex instruction for boys—Juvenile literature.   2. Teenage fathers—
Juvenile literature.   3. Sexual ethics for teenagers—Juvenile literature.
4. Young men—Sexual behavior—Juvenile literature.   5. Masculinity
(Psychology)—Juvenile literature.   6. Teenage pregnancy—Prevention—
Juvenile literature. [1. Sex instruction for boys.   2. Sexual ethics.
3. Masculinity (Psychology)   4. Teenage fathers.]   I. Title.   II. Series.
HQ41.J285 1997
613.9′53—dc20   96-35170
                                                                    CIP
                                                                    AC

Contents

When a father does not take responsibility for his child, the mother is often left to care for the baby by herself.

1 Becoming a Father— Becoming a Man

AT A GROUP ORIENTATION FOR NEWLY HIRED grocery clerks, the manager asks Dominick, age nineteen, "Do you have any children?" "None that I know of," is Dominick's brash response, which is followed by the chuckles and cheers from the other young men seated nearby.

Charles had been a problem at his junior high school. He was constantly getting into fights, and he was eventually expelled for bringing a knife to school. Eight years later he returns to visit his old teachers. He brags, "I'm only twenty-one years old, and I already have three kids by three different mothers."

Jaime is overheard talking to Roger after wrestling practice. "It's her own fault. If she didn't want to get knocked up she would have been on the Pill. If she doesn't want a little Jaime running around, I guess she'll just have to get rid of it."

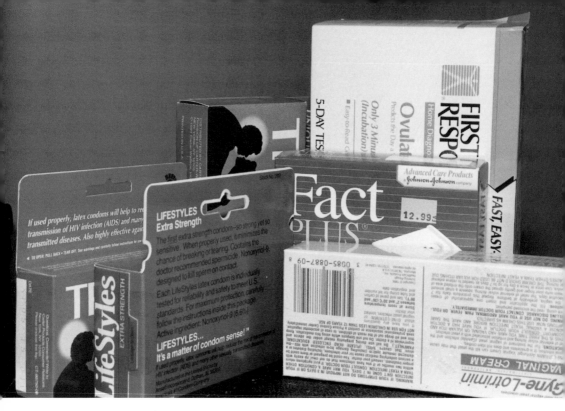

If you choose to be sexually active, there are several ways that you can prevent a pregnancy or a sexually transmitted disease.

Stories like these are repeated every day. Too many young men think that making a girl pregnant makes them more manly. Some brag to anyone who will listen that they are more powerful because they are having unprotected sex. The more danger there is of pregnancy or disease, the more exciting the experience is to many young men.

Births to unmarried teenagers are the responsibility of both the young mother and father. Unfortunately, the burden often falls on the mother because the young father is unwilling to take responsibility for his actions.

The Problem of Teen Pregnancy

The birth rate among teenagers has not changed much over the last thirty years, even with the introduction of birth control, the increase in legal abortion, and fear of AIDS and other sexually transmitted diseases. Each of these factors should tend to keep the unplanned pregnancy rate down, yet the number of teenage pregnancies remains nearly constant. Approximately 1 million teenagers become pregnant each year; more than 530,000 give birth.

Whether or not she chooses to keep the baby, unplanned pregnancy creates a tremendous burden for the teen mother. Although the pregnancy is a result of both parents' actions, the young woman often suffers the most consequences. She is the one who either gives birth to the baby or undergoes an abortion. If she gives birth to the baby, she must either remain responsible for the child for at least eighteen more years or give the baby up for adoption. Keeping the child means losing chances for herself: one in three teen mothers drops out of high school. Making any one of these choices is extremely difficult, especially for a young woman who does not have support from the baby's father.

Whether he realizes it or not, the young father is responsible as well. By law, he must pay for a portion of the care and supplies needed to raise the child, even if he and the mother do not stay together. Being a father means being responsible for bringing a new life into the world. For that reason a father owes his child the best life and as many opportunities as he can possibly provide. This is a huge responsibility for a young man who is trying to figure out his own life and who needs to find a way to support himself. If you become a father before you are ready, you will find your own goals much more difficult to achieve.

Teen fathers are much more likely to be high school dropouts than other male teens. Only 39 percent of teen fathers receive a high school diploma by the age of twenty, compared to 86 percent of male teens who are not fathers. In addition, men who became fathers as teenagers are only half as likely to complete college as men who delayed fatherhood.

2 What It Really Means to Be a Man

EVERY DAY WE HEAR ABOUT WHAT IT MEANS to be a man from our family, our friends, and the media. After a while a young man starts to wonder: What does it really mean to be a man?

Respect and Confidence in Yourself

An important part of being a man is having respect for yourself and confidence in yourself. Feeling inferior and inadequate leads to making poor choices. To overcome these feelings, you need to know who you are and what your strengths are. If you feel that you need more confidence, take out a sheet of paper and list your strong points. Here is an example:

My Strengths:

1. Better than average at math.
2. Can draw well, according to my art teacher.
3. Can swim.
4. Am a good friend to Matt, Jeff, and Chandra.

5. Can run three miles without stopping.
6. Am organized (at least with things that are important to me).
7. Help my parents around the house (usually; sometimes they need to remind me).

By listing your strengths you will gain more appreciation for your good points and more confidence in yourself. In order to respect yourself, you need to know who you are. A person who knows himself will not be tempted to follow the crowd or try to prove that he is "cool." He will be confident and make choices based on reason, rather than insecurity or uncertainty, when he knows who he is, what he believes in, and what he stands for.

Another aspect of being confident is being honest with yourself. Courage comes from facing your fears and weaknesses. It is important to admit to yourself when you feel afraid, overwhelmed, or not good enough. By admitting these feelings, it will be far easier to overcome them. Many young men are sexually active because they hope to overcome these feelings. They find out the hard way that these negative feelings become worse, not better.

Rashid had always been the shortest boy in his class. All of a sudden, in tenth grade, he had a major growth spurt. He became one of the tallest boys. The way girls treated him was a lot different, too. One day Cynthia and her friends came up to him. "You're so nice and tall now, Rashid," Cynthia said. "You're actually pretty cute now." Then all the girls giggled and walked away. Rashid was embarrassed, but he was happy, too. He had always thought Cynthia was beautiful, and she was really popular. She never would have talked to him before. The next weekend, Cynthia invited Rashid over to her house when her parents were away. After talking for hours, they ended up having sex. For Rashid, it was a really special night. He thought he was in love with Cynthia. She was the first girl he had ever slept with.

A few nights later, Cynthia called Rashid and told him that she didn't want to see him anymore. "But I love you!" Rashid protested. Cynthia laughed. "Hey, that wasn't love—that was just sex!" she said and hung up the phone.

Rashid felt terrible. Things got worse a few weeks later when he discovered that Cynthia had given him genital warts. Sex with her had been a big mistake.

Becoming Proactive

People gain confidence and respect for themselves by being proactive, rather than reactive. When you make a choice, ask yourself: Am I doing this because it is what I want to do or because it is what other people want or expect me to do? Being a man means being proactive. It means making your own decisions because you believe that they are right ones. It is important to take other people's needs and wishes into consideration, but ultimately you must do what is right for you.

Setting and Meeting Your Goals

Being a man also means setting and meeting your goals. One important goal is education. Whether your sights are set on completing high school, college, a trade program, or an apprenticeship, it is important to decide what your goal is and then to take the steps needed to reach it.

Another important goal is finding a job and a career. In order to achieve all that you want, you need to find a way to support yourself financially. One of the best ways to find a meaningful career is to identify what things you are good at and enjoy doing. The second step is to figure out what paying job requires these skills and interests. For example, you may enjoy drawing and have some talent for art. Magazines and newspapers sometimes use illustrations to go with stories they publish. By talking to people who need your talents and by getting the education or training you need to improve your skills, you can plan a satisfying career.

Men set and meet personal goals. Your goal may

Identifying your strengths will help you to feel good about yourself and can help to point you toward a career goal.

be to earn an annual salary of $30,000 by the time you are twenty-five years old. Another man may have his sights set on Olympic competition. Another may want to be able to travel around the country or the world. Deciding what your goals are and taking the steps to meet them is an important part of being a man.

For many young men, an unwanted pregnancy can force them to set aside their own goals for the sake of the child and the child's mother. Babies are expensive, and fathers work to support their children. Some fathers avoid their responsibility to their child by abandoning the child and mother. This forces all of the responsibility onto the mother and often the state welfare system. The mother and child will have far fewer opportunities to meet their own goals. This isn't fair. It's also illegal: A father is required by law to support his children. If you're not ready to do this, then you should think about whether you're ready for sex. There is always a chance of pregnancy, even if you use protection.

Respecting Women

Being a man means showing women respect. Respect means that neither person wins or loses, but that decisions are made together. Persuading a woman to do something that she isn't ready to do is tremendously disrespectful.

Respecting women also means continuing to respect yourself. If you are reacting to a woman's wishes, rather than making decisions together, neither of you is showing respect for the other. You cannot develop a mature relationship unless each of you has respect for the other.

Respect requires a great deal of communication. Many young men are not comfortable expressing and sharing emotions. They don't consider it manly to admit weakness or fear. However, listening to a woman's feelings and accepting them are two of the greatest gifts that you can give her. Being unafraid to tell her honestly how you feel is an important part of this gift.

Waiting Until You Are Ready

One aspect of maturity is putting aside what you want now so that you can have a better future. Some young men want it all now. They want money, respect from others, and time to have fun. Unfortunately, there are no shortcuts. People may steal or cheat to get more money; they may physically intimidate others to try to gain respect; they may drop out of school in order to have more free time, but none of these shortcuts really works in the long run. Patience and hard work are needed to meet important goals.

Becoming a father also requires waiting until you are ready. Until a man is ready financially and emotionally, and is in a mature relationship, he is not ready to become a father. Taking a shortcut will usually create problems for the man, his child, and the child's mother.

3 You Are in Charge

YOU ARE PROBABLY BOMBARDED WITH TALK about sex—in school, on TV, with your friends. But who is in control? Will you be a leader or a follower? You have a choice. If you are in control of your own life, you do not do things because they are popular or to help you fit in. If you are in control of your life, you choose to do what you know is right.

Sometimes knowing what is right is hard to figure out. Your body may urge you to do one thing, while your mind is telling you to do something else. What is pleasurable may or may not be right. A real man, mature and responsible, often puts off what would feel good in order to do what he knows is better in the long run. Deciding to wait until you and your partner are ready to become sexually active means that your mind is in control of your body.

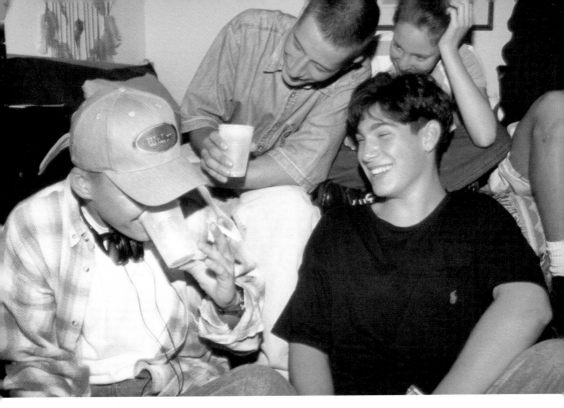
It is much harder to make responsible decisions if you are drinking alcohol or using drugs.

Staying Away from Drugs and Alcohol

Alcohol and drugs impair a person's judgment. While under their influence, a person is likely to do things just because they feel good, without thinking about the long-term consequences. An unwanted pregnancy or sexually transmitted disease (STD), such as AIDS, may be the result of unsafe sexual behavior. In a 1994 study, students who used marijuana, cocaine, other illegal drugs, or alcohol were more likely to report ever having had sexual intercourse, having had multiple sex partners, and not having used a condom during the last sexual intercourse. Because alcohol and drug use can so easily lead to behavior that you would never consider otherwise, it is best to stay away from these sub-stances. The risks are too great: Studies show that almost one-half of unintended pregnancies to teen-agers occur to teens who had been drinking or using drugs.

Knowing Your Limits

Many teenage couples have made a decision not to engage in intercourse until they both feel ready. The excitement and passion of the moment makes it easy to forget their earlier decision, however, and although they regret it later, they may have sex anyway. Unplanned intercourse is far more likely to be unprotected. A study found that 72 percent of teenage girls who planned their first intercourse used contraception, compared to 44 percent of girls who did not plan their first intercourse. Not planning to have sex was cited by teenagers in one study as their top reason for not using contraception. It is also important to remember that pregnancy or STDs can occur even without vaginal intercourse. Oral sex and other kinds of touching are risky activities.

Birth Control: Am I Ready to Be Ready?

By far the best pregnancy prevention is abstinence. If you do choose to be sexually active, however, know the facts and be prepared.

If you decide to be sexually active, you can protect yourself and your partner by using condoms and other methods of birth control.

It is far better to be prepared by providing birth control and discussing pregnancy prevention with your girlfriend than to find yourself in a situation where you engage in unprotected sex. If you plan to be sexually active, it is important to know how and where to obtain condoms or other birth control methods and to be prepared to use them at the right time.

Many men believe that preventing pregnancy is solely the responsibility of the woman. They believe that since it is the woman who becomes pregnant, she should be the one to worry about birth control. Men who believe this are wrong. It takes a man and a woman to create a child, so each one plays an equal part in pregnancy. That means that both are also responsible for contraception.

Each time a couple engages in sex, both partners should be certain that they have protected themselves from an unwanted pregnancy and STDs. A man who takes responsibility for birth control is showing his partner that he respects what she wants in her life; he is not asking her to risk pregnancy and disease.

Taking responsibility for birth control is also very much to a man's advantage. Unprotected sex leaves both partners vulnerable to sexually transmitted diseases, including Acquired Immunodeficiency Syndrome (AIDS), a disease that has no cure. In addition, unwanted pregnancy involves many legal issues. By law, the father is partially responsible for the financial needs of his child until the child reaches the age of eighteen (twenty-one in some states). Some estimate that the cost of raising a child until age twenty-one is between $250,000 and $500,000. Many young fathers run away from their responsibility to their unplanned child, leaving the burden on the mother, her family, and, most likely, the state welfare system.

Choosing a Method of Birth Control

There are a variety of birth control methods available to men and women. When choosing a method with your partner, it is important to look at the factors of safety, cost, and convenience. If you will not be likely to use a method of birth control because you think it is too messy, embarrassing, expensive, or time-consuming, then you should look at other methods. If you are not prepared to take on this responsibility, then you should reconsider your decision to have sex.

No method of birth control, other than abstinence from sex, is 100 percent effective. While some methods are more effective than others, each carries some risk of failure. Remember, too, that effective protection from pregnancy may not prevent the spread of sexually transmitted diseases, such as Human Immunodeficiency Virus (HIV), the virus that causes AIDS.

If you do choose to have sex, protect yourself and your partner by using condoms. Condoms are the only form of birth control that help protect against sexually transmitted diseases. The condom is also an inexpensive and simple form of birth control. When used properly, it is about 85 percent effective. Condoms are available without a prescription and are sometimes even free at schools or clinics. The condom has few side effects. (Occasionally, it may cause irritation or an allergic reaction.)

You can increase the effectiveness of the condom with the additional use of spermicide. Spermicide

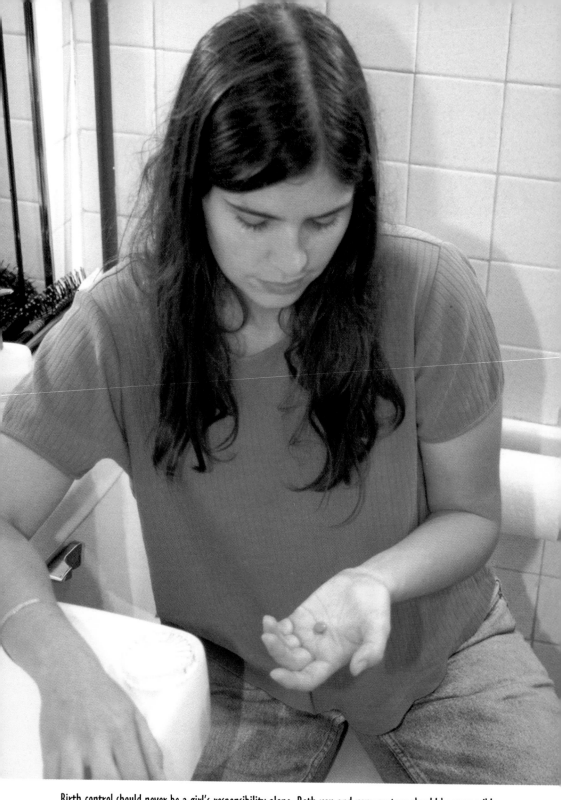

Birth control should never be a girl's responsibility alone. Both you and your partner should be responsible for using birth control if you are sexually active.

comes in the form of creams, foams, tablets, and jellies, and is applied vaginally.

Some types of birth control must be prescribed for a woman by a doctor. These methods include the diaphragm, the cervical cap, Norplant, and the Pill. Even if your girlfriend is using one of these methods, you should still always use condoms when you have intercourse.

Sexually Transmitted Diseases (STDs)

While the focus of this book is pregnancy prevention, it is also every man's responsibility to prevent the spread of STDs. Abstinence is the only 100 percent effective method of preventing the spread of these diseases. If you do choose to be sexually active, protect yourself and your partner with condoms.

Disease can spread rapidly among people. Suppose that over the course of a year a man has sex with five women, each of whom has had sex with five men, each of whom has had sex with five other women. Suddenly, 156 people are involved. If just one of these 156 people had a sexually transmitted disease, it is possible that many of them could become infected with the disease, even though most of the people have not even met each other.

If you suspect that you have a sexually transmitted disease, it is important that you get tested and

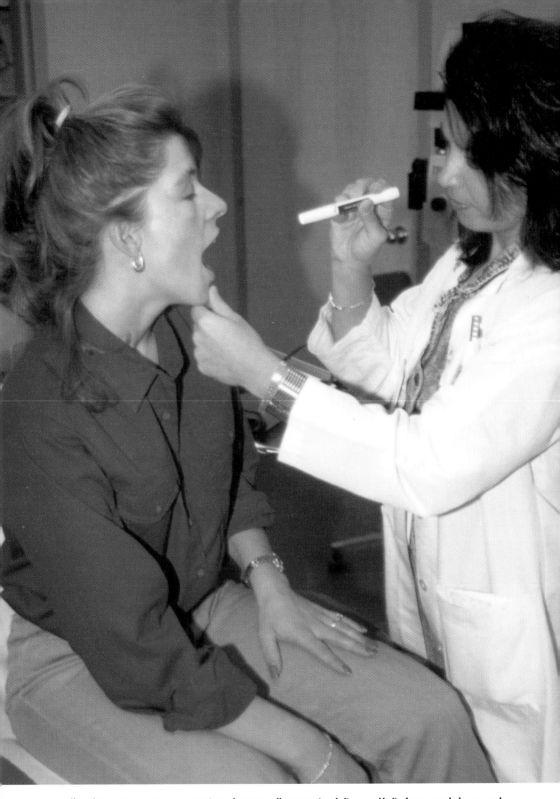

Your doctor can answer your questions about sexually transmitted diseases. Medical care can help you and your girlfriend stay healthy.

treated as soon as possible. There are many free and inexpensive clinics that will do the testing and provide treatment. The results of the testing will not be revealed to anyone except you. These clinics can be found in your local telephone book.

Anyone who contracts a sexually transmitted disease needs to contact each of his or her sexual partners and let them know about the disease. Left untreated, some STDs can leave men and women infertile and—in the case of AIDS—can result in death.

4 A Baby Doesn't Make You a Man

THERE ARE MESSAGES EVERYWHERE TELLING you that sex makes you an adult. It sometimes seems as if a boy cannot be considered a man until he has had sex. Further, some people think that a man cannot truly be considered an adult until he has become a father. These messages that society sends can make young men—and women—feel pressured to become sexually active before they are ready.

Pressure from the Media

Sex is everywhere. Television, movies, and music bombard us with sexual imagery and lyrics. Much of advertising is based on the fact that "sex sells." Newspaper and magazine headlines announce the latest sexual scandals.

Movies are increasingly graphic in the way they portray sex. Characters in films and on television jump into bed with people they have only just met. Sex is often based only on physical attraction; very little is ever said about the importance of

Magazines, TV commercials, and other forms of media frequently emphasize sexual themes.

preventing pregnancy and sexually transmitted diseases such as AIDS. Often the sex depicted onscreen is unprotected.

Television shows become more suggestive with each new season. Nudity is more common. Daytime shows—especially talk shows—focus heavily on topics related to sex. If you watch prime-time television, chances are that you will see roughly three sexual acts per hour. Music videos often depict sexual situations and feature suggestive or explicit language. Some songs celebrate violence and rape. These songs can lead young men to believe that using a woman for a man's pleasure is normal and acceptable, which it is not.

Songs, movies, and TV shows that make unprotected, casual sexual intercourse seem normal are sending the wrong message. Their message—that it is okay to be selfish and irresponsible—ignores the potential real-life consequences of unprotected sex, such as pregnancy or AIDS.

Pressure from Peers

Many teenage boys think that their manliness is measured by how often they have sex and by how many sexual partners they have.

Guys brag about who they were with last night, what they did, and how long they did it. Guys tell stories to top one another. Because they fall for this competition, other guys tell bigger and more elaborate stories. Since no one knows the truth, the storytellers feel that they have proved their manhood. The guys listening to the stories may begin to feel that they don't measure up. To be considered normal, to feel like they fit in, the listeners think that they need to be doing what the other guys are bragging about. What the guys listening to the stories often don't realize is that the stories are usually exaggerated or untrue.

Teenagers develop physically at different rates. Hearing about or seeing the size and development of their peers can make other boys feel badly. To make up for this, a young man may try to have sex more often and with more partners. But respect, responsibility, and self-control are the real marks of masculinity—not one's sexual experiences.

Questions About Sexual Identity

Some young men become so overly concerned with how they measure up sexually that they question their own sexual identity. They think that since they are not having the same or as many sexual experiences as their friends, they might not be heterosexual.

This conclusion comes from combining two pieces of misinformation. The first is that sexual activity makes a boy more manly. We have already seen that this is not true.

The second piece of misinformation is the belief that people become gay because they cannot live up to the demands and expectations of the "straight" world. This concept is completely untrue. Studies have found that sexual identity is determined before birth. Scientists believe that people are naturally attracted to the same or the opposite sex. About 10 percent of all people are homosexual. They don't choose to become homosexual in order to escape the pressures of parenthood and family life or to avoid sex with the opposite sex.

Some men become so threatened by homosexuality that they engage in meaningless heterosexual, or "straight," sex simply to prove to themselves and to the world that they are not gay. These men sometimes use women sexually and often produce children simply to escape their own fears and feelings of not being masculine enough. Being a man means accepting one's sexual identity and acting responsibly.

Pressures from Family

Another source of pressure to have sex and to father a baby can come from family. A young man may feel that he needs to "extend the bloodline" or "carry on the family name." Even without saying it directly, parents can make a young man feel that it is important for him to have children in order to keep the family going. This kind of pressure may make a young man try to become a father before he is ready, in order to gain respect and approval from his parents.

Attempting to keep up with older siblings may be another source of family pressure. If an older brother or sister is receiving a great deal of attention and affection following the birth of his or her child, a younger brother may feel he needs to become a father in order to keep up. If a younger sister becomes pregnant, her older brother may think that he needs to become a parent himself in order to stay ahead of her.

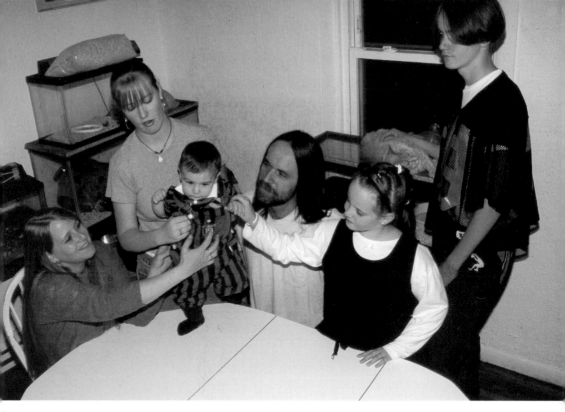

If your sibling has a baby, you may feel like you should become a parent too.

These types of pressures are unreasonable. They are also unfair to the young man's sexual partner. Having sex, and especially having a baby, are joint decisions. When a mature couple decides that they are ready to bring a child into the world, it is because the decision is right for them, not because they want to please their parents or keep up with their siblings. Your family may want you to have a family of your own someday, but they also want you to finish school and find a satisfying career. Focus on these goals, and save starting a family for when you are truly ready.

Some young women may think that having a baby will solve their problems. But often they do not consider how much work and responsibility are involved in raising a child.

Pressures from Girlfriends

A young woman may put pressure on her boyfriend to have sex so that she can have a baby. The attention that friends and sisters receive when they have a baby may make a young woman consider having a baby of her own. Just as a young man may want to keep up with his peers by becoming a father, a young woman may want to become pregnant in order to feel that she is keeping pace with her friends.

A woman may simply have the desire to love and protect a helpless child. She may feel a need to be loved and needed. But babies require a tremendous amount of time, patience, and attention. The work that goes into raising a child has its rewards, of course, but a teen mother may be too overwhelmed and exhausted to enjoy them.

A father is legally responsible for his children even if the mother does not believe that he needs to be. Until both the man and the woman are ready, having a baby is not a mature decision.

If you and your girlfriend are sexually active, and she wants you to stop using birth control so that she can become pregnant, remind her that condoms are the only effective weapon against sexually transmitted diseases. Tell her that you are protecting both of you from catching a disease that could ruin your chances of having a healthy family later in life.

If your girlfriend insists on not using contraception, you can say no to having sex. You may feel nervous about refusing sex with your girlfriend. There is a common assumption that men never turn down sex, and that if they do, it is because they are gay or have something wrong with them. This is not true. A real man knows when to say no to sex. Tell your girlfriend that you are not ready for all the work and money it takes to raise a baby, and that you don't want to get into a situation where you are responsible for one. Once you put it this way, she may reconsider her own wishes. Try to help her understand her real reasons for wanting a baby. Together, maybe you can come up with other solutions to her need to feel loved, such as dealing with an abusive family situation or becoming involved in other activities that will make her feel appreciated.

The Welfare Myth

Sometimes, teens may want to have a baby because a mother below a certain income level receives a welfare check for her child. It is important to remember that the welfare money is meant to be used for the care and feeding of the baby, not as pocket money for the baby's mother or father. In any case, the payment is often barely enough to raise a baby on, much less to profit from.

Baby food and supplies are expensive. Many teen couples receive food stamps and other forms of welfare in order to afford the cost of raising a child.

The welfare system has changed, and teen parents cannot expect that welfare will be there to support them. A welfare check should never be a reason to have a baby, and the baby's father should never expect that he is "owed" part of the money.

5 What It Means to Be a Father

MAKING A WOMAN PREGNANT IS NOT THE same thing as becoming a father. Sexual intercourse can lead to an unplanned pregnancy. Couples finding themselves in this situation generally must decide among three choices: keeping the baby, giving up the baby for adoption, or seeking an abortion. All three choices can be difficult for teens to deal with. Deciding how to handle a pregnancy is not easy.

Keeping the Baby

One of the first options that a young, unmarried, pregnant couple considers is keeping the baby. The first question that they must ask themselves is: Are we ready to either get married or live together? In other words, are we ready to make the commitment and sacrifice that it will take to raise a child together?

In order to answer these questions, the couple needs to first determine whether they can support the child financially. Do they have the resources to provide a home, food, clothing, and medical care for the baby? If not, are they willing to seek help from their parents, the state welfare system, churches, or charitable organizations?

Other important questions the couple should consider are: Are they both ready emotionally to be parents? Are they willing to put in the time and hard work needed to raise a child? Do they have the patience to give up a great deal of their freedom in order to maintain a routine for the baby? Are they willing to be responsible for the day-to-day concerns of a child?

Another consideration for young men is: Are you in a mature relationship with the baby's mother? Do you respect each other? Although the pregnancy was unplanned, is each of you willing to take equal responsibility for the pregnancy? A good way to determine the maturity of your relationship is to ask yourself: Would we be considering marriage and a family if she was not pregnant? If the answer to this question is no, you may not be ready to raise a child together.

Below is a quick questionnaire to help you determine if you are ready to raise a child together. Answer these questions on a separate sheet of paper.

Are We Ready?

1. Do I have the education and job skills to support myself financially and provide a home for my girlfriend and my child? ____Yes____No

2. Does the child's mother have the education and job skills so that she can also earn money and contribute to the child's upbringing? ____Yes____No

3. If we are both working, would we have enough money to pay for child care? ____Yes____No

4. Am I willing to work harder and longer to give my child opportunities? ____Yes____No

5. Am I willing to sacrifice my free time to raise my child? ____Yes____No

6. Can I find the patience to maintain a routine for the baby? ____Yes____No

7. Are both of our families supportive and willing to help us? ____Yes____No

8. Do I respect my girlfriend's hopes, dreams, and goals? ____Yes____No

9. Does my girlfriend respect my hopes, dreams, and goals? ____Yes____No

10. If she was not pregnant already, would we be considering raising a child together? ____Yes____No

If your girlfriend gets pregnant, you will have to decide together whether or not to keep the baby. The final decision should be made by your girlfriend.

If your answer to any of these questions is no, you need to think carefully about whether you are ready to keep and raise a baby together. Many young men are simply not ready to take on the responsibility of raising a child. This is not a measure of weakness or inadequacy; it simply means that the time and the situation are not right.

Sometimes, the mother may decide to keep the baby and raise it on her own. If she makes this choice the father still must provide financial, legal, and emotional support for his child. A child is the responsibility of both parents. Even when the parents are living apart, a man must live up to his obligations.

How much financial support a father provides may be determined by a court. If his earnings are low, it will usually be a set amount of money. If he has greater earning ability, a percentage of his wages, often 20 to 25 percent of all of his income, is set aside for the support of the child. Knowing this, a couple can often reach an agreement on financial support themselves without involving a court.

Many states are becoming more strict about enforcing child-support laws. In Massachusetts, willful nonpayment of child support can land you in prison for as long as five years. In Maine, refusal to pay can result in losing your driver's license.

Legal support involves things such as assisting with educational expenses, providing insurance or medical care, and being responsible for a child who breaks the law. A couple living apart needs to decide the ways that each of these types of support will be provided.

Finally, a father living apart from his child owes him or her emotional support. This means spending time playing with the child and teaching the child about himself or herself and the world as the child grows up. It also means helping the child to find his or her own goals and ways to meet them. It is important to support the child's mother emotionally as well, even if you do not live together.

She has the day-to-day hard work of maintaining the child's routine and providing for the baby's constant needs. It is important to be supportive and appreciative of the care that she is giving to your child.

Adoption

Once a couple has decided that they will not be able to raise the child either together or separately, two options remain: adoption and abortion. Giving a child up for adoption requires a great deal of maturity. Adoption means that the couple has decided that they will allow another family, usually one that they will only meet briefly, to provide a better life for their child than they feel they can.

For a woman to carry a baby for nine months, give birth, and then give up the baby, however, is an extremely difficult experience. To choose adoption, therefore, is also not easy.

Surrendering a child for adoption needs to be a choice with which both of you can live. Unexpected pregnancy is extremely stressful. Giving up a baby for adoption means that both the mother and the father need to agree and to support each other throughout the pregnancy.

A first step to take for a couple seeking to give up a baby for adoption is to find a reputable

Counselors can help you and your girlfriend to make the best decision about a pregnancy.

adoption agency. The best way to find a reputable adoption agency is to ask a doctor, school counselor, social worker, or trusted church leader for a referral. You may want to talk to more than one agency. Most will provide you with medical care at the adoptive parents' expense. The sooner an agency is found, the less expensive the pregnancy will be for the mother and father.

Abortion

If abortion is strictly forbidden by your church or your family, the feelings of guilt following an abortion can be very difficult to deal with. Abortion clinics are required to provide counseling prior to an abortion. It is important that both the mother and father participate in this counseling. Both mother and father either together or separately should schedule a few sessions with a counselor or clinical social worker.

There are several questions to consider. The first question is: Is it too late in the pregnancy already? The safest time for abortion is during the first trimester (three months). Second trimester abortions are more costly and dangerous to the mother. If more than three months have passed, abortion may not be the best alternative.

The second question is: How will you pay for the abortion? Very few states or clinics offer free abortions, though some provide them at low cost. The normal cost of a legal abortion will run from $500 to $1,000. Most of the time, insurance will cover very little of this expense. There is less federal money available for abortion than was available years ago. It is extremely important to find an abortion clinic that is safe, with legitimate, licensed staff. Seek a referral from a doctor or other trusted health professional.

Another question is: Will you need parental consent? Some states require females under eighteen to obtain their parents' permission before undergoing an abortion. (Parental consent is not required to visit a clinic for counseling, however.)

Under most circumstances it is a good idea for a girl under eighteen to make her parents aware of her pregnancy. Although the unplanned pregnancy will probably be difficult for them to accept, their emotional and financial support will help, whatever their daughter and the baby's father decide to do.

If you father a child, you will be faced with many difficult decisions. If you are not ready to face these decisions, having a baby is not a good choice right now.

6 Alternative Sources of Power and Manhood

OUR SOCIETY SENDS MANY MESSAGES WHICH say that sexual activity makes you a man. As we have seen in this book, however, sexual intercourse is a responsible decision only for a couple in a mature relationship who have talked about birth control and STD protection.

Fortunately, many other sources of manhood are available to young men not yet ready to risk their futures for the sake of having sex.

What Is Masculinity?

Masculinity is all of the characteristics that make men unique. In our society, the roles that men and women play are always changing. Women have moved into many formerly male-dominated jobs and leadership roles. Divorce has created many single-parent families. These changes have challenged traditional ideas of the husband who works and the wife who stays at home.

Many men feel relieved that they are less bound

True friends will be interested in and concerned about your thoughts and feelings.

by unreasonable expectations of masculinity. Nobody can be tough, strong, unemotional, and successful all the time.

The definition of masculinity is flexible and personal. What does masculinity mean to you? Think about the men you respect in your life—your father, older brother, an uncle, a teacher, or a coach, for example. What qualities do they have that you admire? You may admire the fact that your uncle put himself through college while working two jobs and supporting a family. Hard work and ambition are important to being a man. So are qualities such as loyalty, patience, and dependability.

There is no denying that men and women are different. Many of these differences, however, are the result of differences in the way boys and girls are raised and taught—that is, the process of socialization. Because of the way they are brought up, young men may find it difficult to be close to other people and share their feelings. They may think that they always have to be tough and strong and keep up with their friends. This can lead them to make some decisions that are not fair to themselves or to the people they care about.

Making more responsible decisions requires having the confidence in yourself to express what you want and feel. Part of developing your own definition of masculinity means being able to talk about the feelings and values that are important to you.

There is a growing movement of men who are learning to explore the meaning of masculinity for themselves. They are open to a new definition of their own masculinity, even if it might be different from what they have been taught.

More and more men are helping each other to overcome the pressures that keep them from forming close friendships with women and other men. Women are often more comfortable expressing their emotions, but men need to talk and cry sometimes, too. Men's groups can provide emotional support and give men an opportunity to share their feelings with other men. Being a man means having the confidence to make your own decisions and to talk to peers or adults you can trust when you need help.

Simon and Lenny had been Paulo's friends for many years. Usually, they would meet after school and go out for burgers, watch a movie, or shoot a game of pool. But for several weeks, Paulo hadn't been much fun to be around. He had been feeling a lot of pressure at home since his father had been laid off. It had become difficult for his parents to afford the things they used to buy. Paulo could tell that the situation upset his father, who would sit around the house all day. It was making Paulo depressed. When he was out with Lenny and Simon, he didn't say much. One day, he didn't feel like going out at all.

"What's with you?" asked Lenny.

Paulo explained the problems that he was having at home. He told his friends about the stress that his father's unemployment caused for the family.

"Who cares?" Lenny replied. "Everybody has problems. Quit being such a baby about it."

Paulo felt pretty embarrassed after that. He had trusted Lenny and Simon with a problem that was bugging him. Their approval was important to him, and now he wasn't sure if he would ever talk to them about personal stuff again. Wasn't there anyone that he could talk with about his feelings? He went home alone and even unhappier than before.

He was surprised when Simon called him that night.

"Listen, I can't believe how Lenny acted today,"
Simon said. *"You know, I went through the same thing with my parents a few years ago. It was a tough time, but things are better now. It does get easier."*

Simon understood what Paulo was going through. They talked for an hour. After they hung up, Paulo felt less alone.

Exploring Your Masculinity

There are many ways that a boy can learn to develop into a man. Some of the best ways to develop your own sense of masculinity are: getting involved in activities that will help you to learn how to set and meet your own goals, developing friendships with young women, and seeking the advice and influence of men in your family or community.

One way to learn how to set and meet your own personal goals is through athletics. Sports allow you to improve and excel at a physical activity. Each competition allows you to set your goals and expectations higher than the time before. The training and practice necessary for sports helps athletes to develop the patience and discipline needed to meet long-term goals.

Sports are not for everybody, though. School clubs and student government can help develop the same skills, as well as the important skills of leadership and negotiation. Learn how to achieve positive change and how to plan and manage events. Motivate others to work toward a goal. Getting involved in church youth groups, musical and dramatic productions, the Boy Scouts, and volunteer opportunities all can help you learn to be responsible, dependable, committed, and confident. Do you hope to be a doctor someday? Talk to your own doctor about volunteering in a hospital or clinic. Are you more interested in becoming an auto technician? Talk to someone in the field. Try to set up an apprenticeship.

Taking on a part-time job will help you learn to balance school, work, and hobbies. Are you interested in the computer field? Find part-time work in a computer store to get the experience you need.

Part-time workers often have to miss other activities because they are scheduled to work. Putting off immediate pleasure for a long-term reward is a reflection of maturity. A part-time job might also allow you to explore the types of work you would like to eventually pursue for your career.

Developing Friendships with Women

Roland had a part-time job working at a fast-food

restaurant. He liked the extra cash and the people he worked with, many of whom were his age. One of the other workers was Sonia. Sonia and Roland would often work the same shift. During the evenings, when they closed up the restaurant together, they talked about school or their families or whatever else was on their minds. Roland felt comfortable talking to Sonia. She trusted him with her thoughts, too.

One afternoon Roland was working with his friend Carlos. When they were on their break, Carlos asked Roland about Sonia.

"So, I noticed you hanging around with Sonia," Carlos said. "She's pretty cute. What's up with the two of you?"

Roland laughed. "It's nothing like that at all," he said. "She's just a friend."

Carlos's comment made Roland think about his relationship with Sonia. It was so much easier to talk with her than with most of the other girls at school. They made him feel nervous and embarrassed. Maybe it was because he was usually thinking more about their looks than about what they actually had to say. But because he had gotten to know her as more than a pretty girl, Roland felt no need to impress Sonia. He liked talking with her and trusted her as a friend. He could really relax and be comfortable around her. Roland realized that maybe what his dad said was true: that a girl's looks mattered less than the kind of person she was.

Work on developing friendships with some of the girls you know.

Another important part of becoming a man is to learn to develop healthy and respectful friendships and relationships with women. Start by going to school dances together, dating, and talking on the telephone. As you learn to become a man, you will realize that communication and respect are far more important than sex in relationships with women. Get to know women as people. When you meet a girl you like, think of her as a potential friend, not just a potential girlfriend.

Finding Role Models

Even when he was a small boy, Edwin had been fasci-nated with cars and mechanics. Now he had to admire his friends' cars because he didn't have enough money for one of his own. He was good at fixing things, but he didn't know enough to be hired at a garage. His uncle Hobart knew about Edwin's interest and offered to introduce him to his friend Santiago who owned a garage only a few blocks away. When they met, Edwin agreed to work as Santiago's apprentice. At first, that usually meant helping in the office. But the longer he was in Santiago's garage, the more he learned about mechanics.

Santiago had owned his garage for many years. Everybody knew about Santiago and his garage. But it wasn't always that way. Sometimes Santiago told Edwin about how he used to work in other garages around town, or with a pit crew at the auto races. He had to take many other jobs in order to save up enough money to buy his own garage. It was a goal that took a lot of time and work to achieve.

Edwin admired the pride that Santiago took in his work. He admired how Santiago worked hard to buy his own garage. Edwin enjoyed talking with Santiago and was fascinated by all of his old stories. Sometimes Edwin talked about the things going on in his life. He respected Santiago's advice.

Another way to learn to be a man is to get to know and understand men in your family and your community. Choose positive role models. Do you admire an uncle or older cousin? Do you respect a neighbor who has a good job in your field of interest? Try to spend more time with these people. By listening to and asking questions of men who are successful, you will learn what goals you want to set for yourself. Many schools and community centers have mentoring programs. Talk to your school counselor or a teacher about how you can get involved in one of these programs.

It is especially important to find a positive role model when you are not close to your father. This may be the case if your father does not live with you. Even if your father is around, he may not "be there" for you emotionally.

The person you admire can be unlike many of the other men around you. He should be someone who has the qualities you respect most.

Where to Go When You Need Help

Sometimes it's hard to know where to start. The teenage years are very confusing. The rules seem to change constantly. It is difficult to know where to turn when you are confused. Getting the help you need is an important and mature step.

The first place to try is right at home. Parents and older siblings can be great resources. Ask them what they do when they are confused or need direction. They may have surprising ideas. Uncles, grandfathers, and close family friends can also be very helpful when you need to sort things out.

There are also many helpful resources at school. Guidance counselors, social workers, and school nurses are all trained to give you help. You might also approach a teacher or coach.

Another place to turn for advice is your church, synagogue, mosque, or other place of worship. All of these institutions have staff who are trained to help answer life's most difficult questions.

If you are still confused and need more help, you may want to call or write one of the organizations listed at the back of this book.

Remember: The road to becoming a man requires courage, patience, and confidence in yourself. You can do it if you think things through ahead of time and trust yourself.

Glossary

abortion A medical procedure for ending a pregnancy. Usually performed during the first three months of pregnancy.

abstinence Choosing not to participate in sexual intercourse.

adoption Transferring all legal claim to and responsibility for a child to a parent or guardian other than a child's natural mother or father.

AIDS (Acquired Immunodeficiency Syndrome) A fatal disease of the body's immune system. AIDS is transmitted through bodily fluids exchanged during activities such as unprotected sex and sharing infected hypodermic needles.

birth control Any substance or device that makes pregnancy less likely. The most common methods are condoms and birth control pills.

confidence A belief in oneself and one's ability to set and meet goals.

contraception Birth control.

emotional support Being there for others by listening, communicating, and spending time with them.

financial support Providing money for food, shelter, clothing, education, and medical care.

heterosexual An attraction to members of the opposite sex.

HIV (Human Immunodeficiency Virus) The virus that causes AIDS.

homosexual An attraction to members of the same sex.

legal support Meeting obligations to a child and the mother as provided by law.

masculinity The characteristics of manhood.

maturity The ability to set aside immediate pleasure in view of long-term benefits and/or consequences.

patience The ability to wait and set goals for the future.

respect Accepting another person while allowing that person to set his or her own goals and meet his or her own needs.

responsibility Following through on commitments and dealing with difficulties when you have played a part in them.

self-control Doing what a person knows is right, rather than what he wants or what others would like him to do.

STD (sexually transmitted disease) Any disease that can be spread through sexual intercourse or other sexual activities.

Help List

Big Brothers Big Sisters of America
230 North 13th Street
Philadelphia, PA 19107
(215) 567-7000
e-mail: bbbsa@aol.com
Web site: http://www.bbbsa.org

Boys and Girls Clubs of America
1230 West Peachtree Street NW
Atlanta, GA 30309-3447
(404) 815-5740

National Institute for Responsible Fatherhood
8555 Hough Avenue
Cleveland, OH 44108
(216) 791-1468

National Urban League
500 East 62nd Street
New York, NY 10021
(212) 310-9000

Planned Parenthood Federation of America
810 Seventh Avenue
New York, NY 10019
(212) 541-7800
e-mail: communications@ppfa.org
Web site: http://www.ppfa.org/ppfa/

Youth Service USA
3245 Central Avenue
Memphis, TN 38111
(901) 320-1020

In Canada:
Planned Parenthood Federation of Canada
1 Nicholas Street, Suite 430
Ottawa, Ontario K1N 7B7
(613) 241-4474

For Further Reading

Arthur, Shirley. *Surviving Teen Pregnancy: Your Choices, Dreams, and Decisions.* Buena Park, CA: Morning Glory Press, 1991.

Betcher, William, and William Pollack. *In a Time of Fallen Heroes: The Re-creation of Masculinity.* New York: Atheneum, 1993.

Gravelle, Karen, and Leslie Peterson. *Teenage Fathers.* New York: Julian Messner, 1992.

Kuklin, Susan. *What Do I Do Now?: Talking About Teenage Pregnancy.* New York: Putnam, 1991.

Ross, John Munder. *What Men Want: Mothers, Fathers, and Manhood.* Cambridge, MA: Harvard University Press, 1994.

Wood, Samuel G. *Everything You Need to Know About Sexually Transmitted Disease,* rev. ed. New York: Rosen Publishing Group, 1994.

Index

About the Author

Raymond Jamiolkowski received a B.A. in elementary education and an M.A. in guidance and counseling from Northern Illinois University, DeKalb. He taught grades two, five, and six, and has since worked as a guidance counselor.

Mr. Jamiolkowksi lives in Naperville, Illinois, with his wife, Mel, his daughter, Jenny, and his son, David.

Photo Credits

Cover by Ira Fox; page 29 by Michael Brandt; all other photos by Ira Fox.

Layout and Design

Erin McKenna